Our Senses

TASTE

Kay Woodward

GARETH**STEVENS**
GS
PUBLISHING
A World Almanac Education Group Company

Please visit our web site at: **www.garethstevens.com**
For a free color catalog describing Gareth Stevens Publishing's list of high-quality books and multimedia programs, call 1-800-542-2595 (USA) or 1-800-387-3178 (Canada). Gareth Stevens Publishing's fax: (414) 332-3567.

Library of Congress Cataloging-in-Publication Data

Woodward, Kay.
    Taste / Kay Woodward.
       p. cm — (Our senses)
    Includes index.
    ISBN 0-8368-4409-2 (lib. bdg.)
    1. Taste—Juvenile literature. I. Title.
    QP456.W66   2005
    612.8'7—dc22   2004052571

This North American edition first published in 2005 by
Gareth Stevens Publishing
A World Almanac Education Group Company
330 West Olive Street, Suite 100
Milwaukee, Wisconsin 53212 USA

This U.S. edition copyright © 2005 by Gareth Stevens, Inc.
Original edition copyright © 2005 by Hodder Wayland.
First published in 2005 by Hodder Wayland, an imprint of
Hodder Children's Books, a division of Hodder Headline
Limited, 338 Euston Road, London NW1 3BH, U.K.

Commissioning Editor: Victoria Brooker
Book Editor: Katie Sergeant
Consultant: Carol Ballard
Picture Research: Katie Sergeant
Book Designer: Jane Hawkins
Cover: Hodder Children's Books

Gareth Stevens Editor: Barbara Kiely Miller
Gareth Stevens Designer: Kami Koenig

Printed in China

1 2 3 4 5 6 7 8 9 09 08 07 06 05

Picture Credits
Corbis: imprint page, 17 (RNT Productions), 10 (Richard
Hutchings), 12 (Owen Franken), 16 (Danny Lehman), 18
(Francine Fleischer), 19, 22 (right) (Royalty-Free), 20
(Richard Cummins); Getty Images: cover (Stone/Cheryl
Maeder), title page, 11 (left) (Photodisc Green/SW
Productions/Royalty-Free), 4 (Stone/Paul Harris), 5
(Stone/Dave Nagel), 8 (Photodisc Green/SW
Productions/Royalty-Free), 9 (Photodisc Green/Buccina
Studios/Royalty-Free), 13 (Stone/James Darell), 14 (Taxi/
Greg Ceo), 15 (FoodPix/John E Kelly); NHPA: 21 (N.A.
Callow); Wayland Picture Library: 7, 11 (right), 22 (left),
23 (both). Artwork on page 6 is by Peter Bull.

About the Author

Kay Woodward is an experienced children's author who
has written over twenty nonfiction and fiction titles.

About the Consultant

Carol Ballard is an elementary school science
coordinator. She is the author of many books for
children and is a consultant for several publishers.

CONTENTS

Tastes Everywhere!   4

How Your Tongue Works   6

Flavor   8

Sweet, Salty, Sour, and Bitter   10

Taste and Smell   12

Hot and Cold Foods   14

Flavors around the World   16

Animals and Taste   18

Insects and Taste   20

Do You Like How It Tastes?   22

Glossary and Index   24

Words in **bold** type can be found in the glossary.

TASTES EVERYWHERE!

The world has all kinds of delicious foods and drinks for us to enjoy. Our **sense** of **taste** tells us what we like to eat and drink. Sometimes, our sense of taste helps us know if food is safe to eat.

What fruits and vegetables do you like to eat?

This boy likes the taste of ice cream!

We use our tongues to taste. We can taste food by licking it or by putting it into our mouths.

HOW YOUR TONGUE WORKS

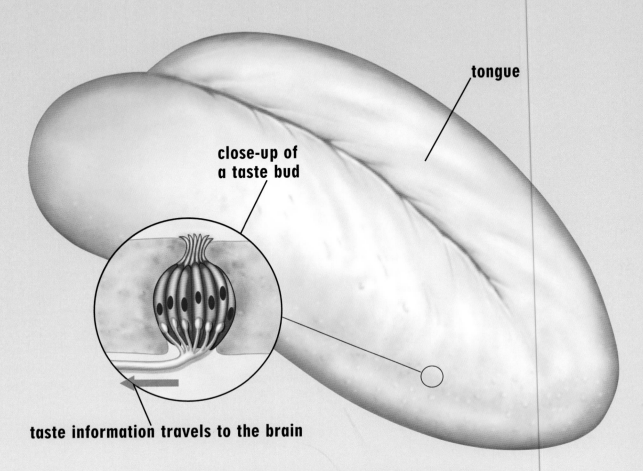

tongue

close-up of
a taste bud

taste information travels to the brain

There are thousands of taste
buds all over your tongue.

Your tongue is covered with lots of tiny bumps called
taste buds. When your tongue touches food, its taste
buds send information about the food to your brain.
This information, along with the smell of the food, helps
your brain know what the food is and if you like it.

Your mouth makes a liquid called **saliva**. When food is very dry, your mouth makes more saliva. The extra saliva makes tasting and eating the dry food easier.

Saliva helps you swallow dry food, such as crackers.

FLAVOR

Flavor is what food tastes like. Different kinds of foods have different flavors. Strawberries, lemons, pizza, and fish all have different flavors.

Foods have thousands of different flavors. People can make tasty meals by mixing together foods with different flavors.

SWEET, SALTY, SOUR, AND BITTER

The taste buds on your tongue can taste four main flavors — sweet, salty, sour, and bitter.

Chocolate has a sweet taste, but lemons are sour.

Honey and chocolate taste sweet. Peanuts and potato chips taste salty. Lemons and yogurt taste sour. Radishes and broccoli taste bitter.

TASTE AND SMELL

Our sense of taste and sense of smell work together. If you like the smell of a food or drink, you will probably like the taste of it, too.

When you have a cold and your nose is stuffed up, it may be difficult for you to smell and taste food. The senses of smell and taste often grow weaker in people as they get older, too.

HOT AND COLD FOODS

Some foods taste better when they are served hot.
Many people like to drink hot cocoa, coffee, tea,
or soup when the weather is cold. A hot drink or
hot food makes people feel warmer on the inside.

Some foods taste better when they are served cold. A chilled drink and a cold salad make a perfect meal on a hot day. Some foods taste good when they are served either hot or cold.

FLAVORS AROUND THE WORLD

Different flavors and foods are popular in different countries around the world. In Italy, many people like to eat pizza and pasta. In Mexico, hot and spicy foods are popular.

You can eat foods from all around
the world in your own home!

Today, more and more people travel to other places in the world. When visiting **foreign** countries, many people enjoy eating new foods with different flavors. After coming home, they may learn to cook these foods or eat them in restaurants.

ANIMALS AND TASTE

Many animals can taste different flavors. Dogs can taste sweet things, but some sweet foods, such as chocolate, are not good for dogs to eat. Cats cannot taste sweet things at all.

Some underwater creatures do not taste with their tongues. Catfish have skin and special whiskers that are covered with taste buds. Octopuses taste their food with the ends of their eight **tentacles**.

INSECTS AND TASTE

Like people, many insects can taste foods in their mouths, but some insects taste with other body parts. Blowflies and butterflies taste with their feet.

Honeybees taste their food with the tips of their **antennae**. Bees can find out what different foods taste like before eating them.

DO YOU LIKE HOW IT TASTES?

1. Find out if you like the same flavors that your friends and family like. Ask an adult to help you gather different types of sweet, salty, sour, and bitter foods and drinks. For example:

Sweet

bananas

candy

soda pop

Salty

olives

peanuts

potato chips

Sour

grapefruits

lemons

yogurt

Bitter

broccoli

radishes

tonic water

2. Ask your friends and family to smell each kind of food and drink. Did they like the smells?

3. Now ask everyone to taste each kind of food and drink. Did they like the flavors?

You may find that when people liked the smell of a food or drink, they also liked its taste. This is because the senses of smell and taste are linked.

Now ask everyone which flavors they liked the best. Did everyone like the same foods and drinks? Which flavors were the most popular? Were any flavors unpopular?

GLOSSARY

antennae: the long, thin body parts that stick out of an insect's head

flavor: the blend of taste and smell sensations caused by a substance in the mouth

foreign: outside of or from a country other than your own

saliva: a liquid made by your mouth to help you eat food

sense: a natural ability to receive and process information using one or more of the body's sense organs, such as the ears, eyes, nose, tongue, or skin. The five senses are hearing, sight, smell, taste, and touch.

taste: (n) the flavor of a substance or the sweet, salty, sour, or bitter quality of a substance identified by the sense of taste; the sense used to receive and identify the flavors of foods and drinks; (v) to figure out the flavor of a food or drink by putting some into the mouth

taste buds: tiny bumps on the tongue that taste substances and send messages to the brain to help identify the substances

tentacles: long, flexible parts that stick out from the bodies of some sea animals and are used for grasping and sometimes tasting

INDEX

animals 18–19

brain 6

eating 4, 7, 16, 17, 21

flavors 8, 9, 10, 16, 18
    bitter 10, 11, 22
    salty 10, 11, 22
    sour 10, 11, 22
    sweet 10, 11, 18, 22

foods 4, 5, 6, 7, 8, 9, 11, 12, 13, 14, 15, 16, 17, 19, 20, 21, 22, 23

insects 20–21

meals 9, 15
mouths 5, 7, 20

noses 13

senses 4, 12, 13, 23
smelling 13, 23
smells 6, 12, 13, 23

taste buds 6, 10, 19
tastes 4, 5, 6, 7, 8, 11, 12, 13, 22, 23
tasting 5, 6, 10, 11, 13, 14, 15, 18, 19, 20, 21, 23
tongues 5, 6, 10, 19